Helping Children See Jesus

ISBN: 978-1-933206-74-5

THE HOLY SPIRIT
New Testament Volume 14
Acts Part 1

Author: Ruth B. Greiner
Illustrator: Frances H. Hertzler
Computer Graphic Artist: Ed Olson
Typesetting and Layout: Morgan Melton, Patricia Pope

© 2018 Bible Visuals International
PO Box 153, Akron, PA 17501-0153
Phone: (717) 859-1131
www.biblevisuals.org

All rights reserved. No part of this publication may be reproduced, stored in a retrieval system or transmitted in any form by any means, electronic, mechanical, photocopy, recording or otherwise, without the prior permission of the publisher, except as provided by USA copyright law.

RELATED ITEMS

To access related items (such as activities, memory verse posters and translated texts) please visit our web store at www.biblevisuals.org and enter 1014 at the top right of the web page. You may need to reduce the zoom setting to get the search box.

FREE TEXT DOWNLOAD

To obtain a FREE printable copy of the English teaching text (PDF format) under Product Format, please scroll down and select Extra–PDF Teacher Text Download. Then under Language select English before clicking the ADD TO CART button to place in your shopping cart. Other languages are available at an additional cost from the Language menu. When checking out, use coupon code XTACSV17 at checkout and click on Apply Coupon to receive the discount on the English text.

A
B
C

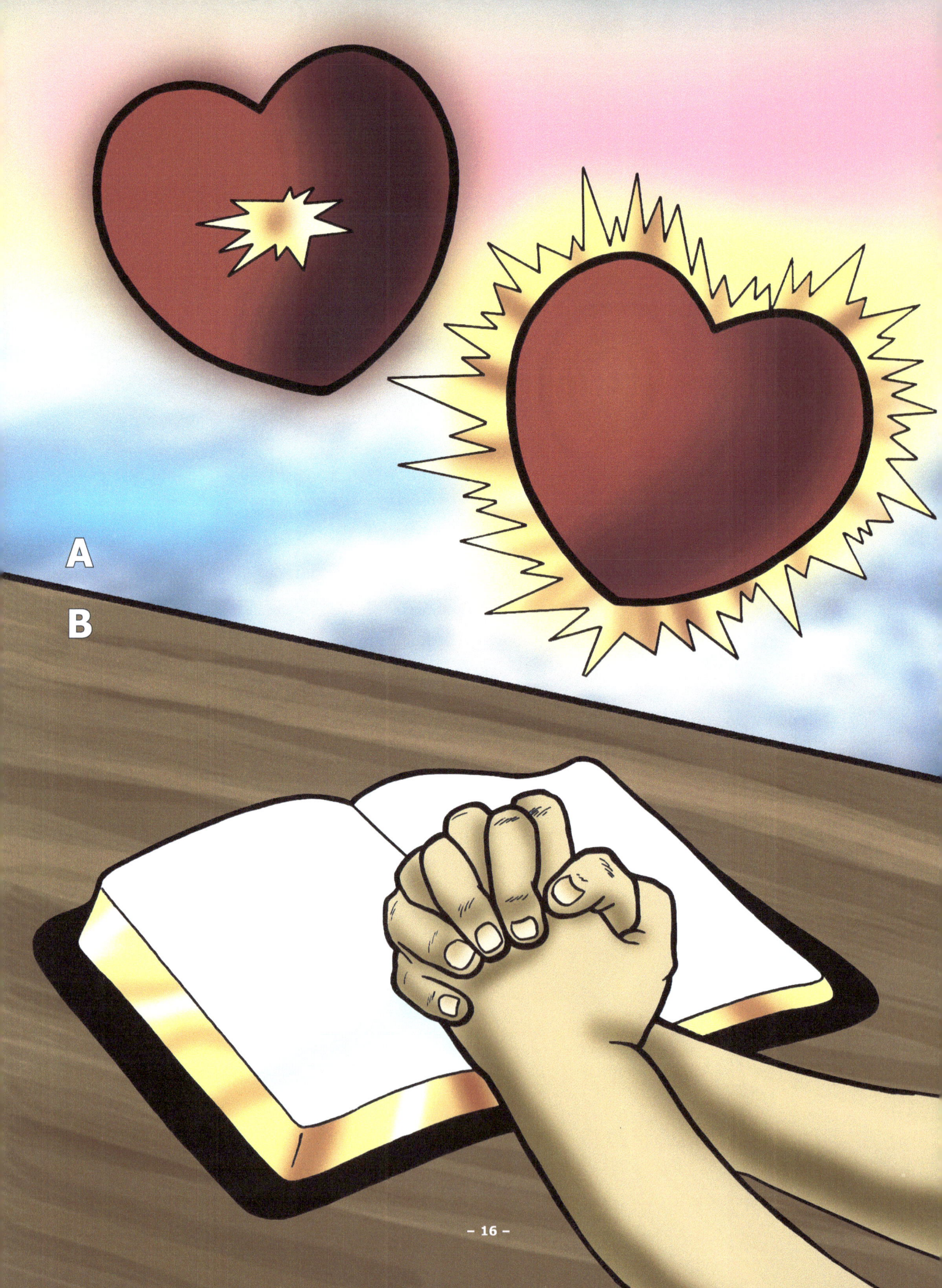

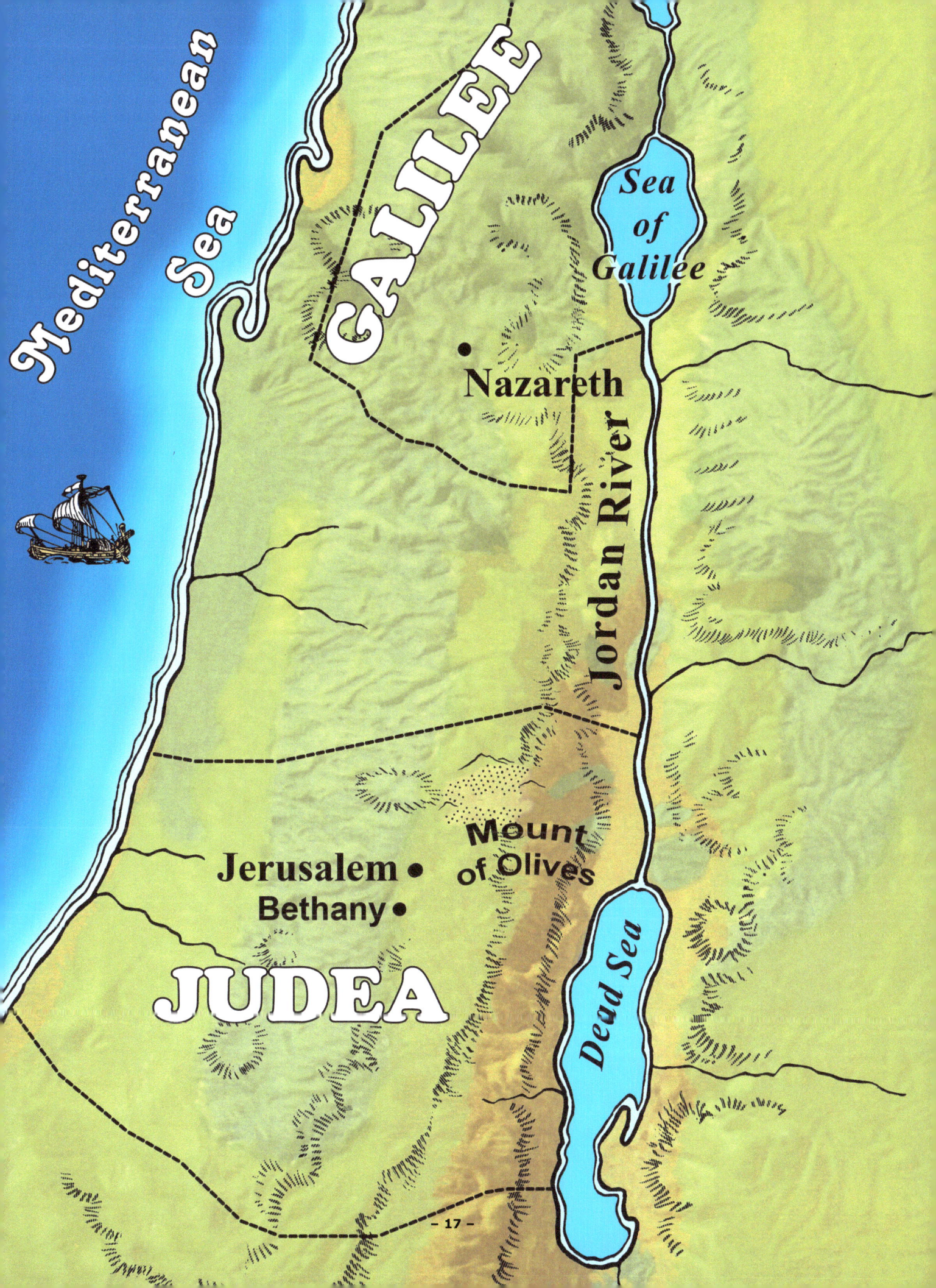

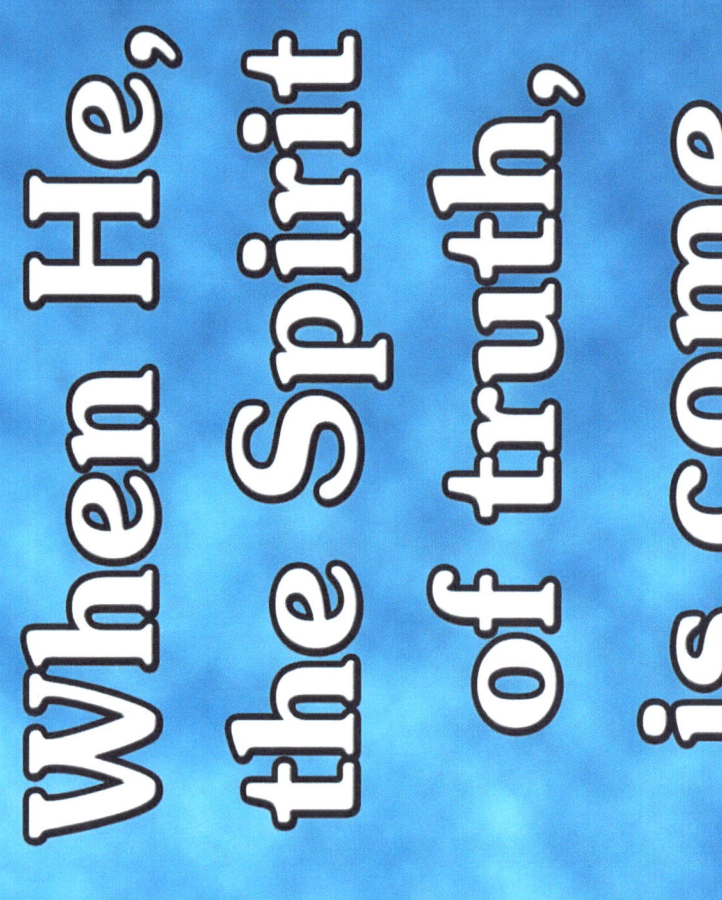

"When He, the Spirit of truth, is come, He will guide you into all truth . . ." John 16:13a

Lesson 1
THE PROMISE OF HIS COMING

Scripture to be studied: Matthew 28:16-20; Mark 16:15-20; Luke 24:49-53; John 14:1-3; John 16:7-33; Acts 1:1-12; Joel 2:28-29

The *aim* of the lesson: To teach that Christ promised to send the Holy Spirit to help believers until He returns.

What your students should *know*: Those who have trusted in Jesus Christ are responsible to tell others of Him.

What your students should *feel*: A desire to be witnesses of Jesus.

What your students should *do*: Believe that Jesus is the Son of God, that He died for their sins and receive Him as their Saviour.

Lesson outline (for the teacher's and students' notebooks):
1. Jesus promises to send the Holy Spirit (John 14:16-17; 16:7).
2. The disciples are given new work (Matthew 28:19-20).
3. Jesus returns to Heaven (Acts 1:9).
4. Angels promise that Christ will return (Acts 1:10-11).

The verse to be memorized:

When He, the Spirit of truth, is come, He will guide you into all truth. (John 16:13a)

> **NOTE TO THE TEACHER**
>
> This lesson will serve as a bridge between the first four books of the New Testament and the fifth book–Acts. The Gospel writers recorded the things that Jesus began to do and to teach until He was received up into Heaven. The book of Acts reviews the things He began to do after He was received up. He has never ceased doing things. His work is still going on. It continues through His true disciples, including you and me. By His presence and the power of the Holy Spirit, Christ works through you, dear teacher. What an honor and privilege to be called as His spokesman, His servant!

THE LESSON

Before His crucifixion, the Lord Jesus had explained to His disciples that He would have to leave them. He would die and rise again, He said. And He told them that sometime after His resurrection from the dead, He would return to His Father in Heaven. (See John 14:28.) The disciples were sad about that for they wanted Jesus to stay with them forever.

Jesus explained two of the reasons for His returning to Heaven. He said, "I go to prepare a place for you. And if I go and prepare a place for you, I will come again and receive you to Myself, that you can be with Me where I am." (See John 14:1-3; compare 1 Thessalonians 4:13-18.) That was a great promise! Jesus would go away for a while and would get a place ready for the disciples so that they would live with Him forever. That news must have cheered them.

1. JESUS PROMISES TO SEND THE HOLY SPIRIT
John 14:16-17; 16:7

But Jesus had another reason for returning to Heaven. He explained it this way, "If I go away, I will send you another Helper *just like Myself*. He will be forever with you and in you. But I cannot send Him until I return to My Father in Heaven. This is why I must leave you." (See John 14:16-17; 16:7.)

The person who would come, of whom God the Son spoke, was God the Holy Spirit.

Show Illustration #1

There were doubtless many times after the death and resurrection of Christ that the disciples talked together about the Promised One who was to come. They would have remembered that when God the Son came to earth, He came as a baby. Angels and a star announced His coming. But how would God the Holy Spirit come to earth? A spirit does not have a body. How would they know He had come? How would His coming be announced?

Perhaps one or two of the disciples explained to the others that once before, God the Father had opened the heavens, and God the Holy Spirit had come down like a dove upon God the Son. (See John 1:32. This had taken place three years earlier at the baptism of the Lord Jesus.) Before that happened, God had told John the Baptist that the One upon whom he would see the Spirit descending would be the Son of God. So, when John the Baptist saw that happen, he exclaimed, "This is the Son of God!" (See John 1:33-40.) (*Teacher:* You may wish to help your students to remember this event by showing Illustration #5 of Volume Two.)

Would God the Holy Spirit again come in the form of a dove? The puzzled disciples probably decided that since the Lord Jesus had told them that the Holy Spirit would be within them (and all believers), He would be everywhere at once. Only a spirit could be everywhere at once. But if they could not see Him, how could they be certain that He had come?

2. THE DISCIPLES ARE GIVEN NEW WORK
Matthew 28:19-20

Show Illustration #2

After His resurrection, the Lord Jesus met again with His disciples. They bowed before Him and worshiped Him, God the Son. He told them, "All power in Heaven and on earth has been given to Me." *All* power! They remembered how He had used His glorious power: He enabled cripples to walk; He gave sight to the blind; He even raised the dead to life. But strangely enough He had not used His great power to keep Himself from suffering or from death. He could have stopped the wicked men from nailing Him to the cross. But He chose not to do so, for His time had come to suffer and to die for sinners. But now He was alive forevermore and *all* power was His.

Having told the disciples that He had all power, He added, "You go to the whole world. Make disciples of all nations." This was to be their new work. They were to be missionaries. They were to tell the good news of salvation to the world. They were to tell about His life on earth, His death and His resurrection so that men and women and children of every land could know about Him and be given the opportunity to believe in Him.

To comfort His disciples, Jesus said, "I am always with you." And He reminded them how He would always be with them by saying, "I will send the Holy Spirit–just as My Father promised. Do not begin telling others about Me yet. Stay in the city of Jerusalem until He comes and fills you with power from Heaven." Only then would His power be their power.

Forty days after His resurrection, Jesus led His disciples toward Bethany, to the Mount of Olives, just outside the city of Jerusalem. And again He promised, "When the Holy Spirit has come upon you, you will have power. You will have power to speak in My Name about My death and resurrection. You will tell this good news to people in Jerusalem, and in Judea, and in Samaria, and to the farthest parts of the earth!"

3. JESUS RETURNS TO HEAVEN
Acts 1:9

Show Illustration #3

Then the most amazing thing happened! He began to go up into the air. Higher and higher He went. The disciples gazed in unbelief. He was going back to Heaven to be with God the Father. And they were seeing it happen–seeing it with their very own eyes! They watched, even after He had disappeared in a cloud. He was gone!

4. ANGELS PROMISE THAT CHRIST WILL RETURN
Acts 1:10-11

Show Illustration #4

Suddenly two men in white robes stood beside the disciples. "Men of Galilee," the visitors said, "why are you looking up into Heaven? This same Jesus who was taken up from you into Heaven will come back in the same way that you saw Him go into Heaven."

This news made the disciples glad. They bowed and worshiped Jesus even though they could not see Him. And, remembering the command of the Lord Jesus, they returned to Jerusalem with joy to wait for the coming of the Holy Spirit. (See Luke 24:52.) They did not know exactly when He would come. The Lord Jesus had not told them.

Far away from the city of Jerusalem, far, far away from earth, the Lord Jesus Christ, in His resurrected body, arrived in the very presence of God the Father in Heaven. What a glorious meeting that must have been! Thousands upon thousands of angels were there to welcome and worship God the Son who had gone to earth for about 33 years to live–and to die for sinners. Because of that great sacrifice, millions of men and women and boys and girls would believe in Christ Jesus as Saviour, and so would someday live with Him and His Father forever.

Are you one of those who will live with Him in Heaven someday? If you believe that He is the Son of God, if you believe He died for your sins, if you have received Him as your Lord and Saviour, you can be certain of living with Him!

Lesson 2
THE COMING OF THE HOLY SPIRIT

NOTE TO THE TEACHER

Do you realize that the work you are doing for God is the same work that the apostles were commanded to do? The Holy Spirit who came to live in and empower the apostles, is the One who lives within you and gives you power to do His work. The Holy Spirit is as powerful as He was in the days of the apostles.

The coming of the Holy Spirit at Pentecost fulfilled the promise Jesus had made to His followers. He had promised to ask the Father to send the Comforter, the Holy Spirit, to be with and in believers. At Pentecost the apostles realized that the Lord Jesus was indeed at the throne of His Father in Heaven and that He had kept His word.

Scripture to be studied: Acts 1:13-26; 2:1-41; Leviticus 23:15-22

The *aim* of the lesson: To show that the promise Jesus made concerning the coming of the Holy Spirit was fulfilled at Pentecost.

What your students should *know*: The Holy Spirit lives in each believer and desires to work through each one.

What your students should *feel*: A desire to be strong witnesses for Christ.

What your students should *do*: Ask the Lord to help them tell someone about the Lord Jesus Christ this week.

Lesson outline (for the teacher's and students' notebooks):
1. Believers wait for the Holy Spirit (Acts 1:4).
2. The Holy Spirit fills believers (Acts 2:1-4).
3. Believers, filled with the Holy Spirit, witness powerfully (Acts 2:5-13).
4. Many people turn to Christ (Acts 2:14-41).

The verse to be memorized:

When He, the Spirit of truth, is come, He will guide you into all truth. (John 16:13a)

THE LESSON

Jesus had gone away to Heaven. The disciples obediently returned to Jerusalem where they met together in an upstairs room of a house. They could scarcely wait to begin their great work for God, as Jesus had commanded them. They were eager to tell everyone in Jerusalem that the One who had been crucified had proved that He was truly the Son of God by rising from the dead. They longed to spread the news that God the Son had died to bring salvation to all who would believe in Him. They wanted other disciples to join them in spreading the message of salvation through Judea and Samaria and to every country in the world.

For three years the disciples had been prepared by Jesus for this great new work. They had been learners. (The word *disciple* means "learner.") But now they would be apostles. (*Apostles* means "sent ones.") Jesus had told them that He was sending them into all the world to spread the good news that He had died for the sin of the world and had risen from the dead. His disciples knew and understood these truths. Now they who had learned would go out to tell what they knew. They would be His witnesses.

1. BELIEVERS WAIT FOR THE HOLY SPIRIT
Acts 1:4

But as eager as these men were to do their new work, they could not go. The Lord Jesus had commanded them to wait in Jerusalem for the Holy Spirit who would come and give them strength and power to do the tremendous work that He wanted them to do.

Show Illustration #5

Others joined the apostles. The brothers of Jesus were there. Mary, the mother of Jesus, and some other women were with them in the room. While they waited for the coming of the Holy Spirit, they prayed. Altogether there were about 120 people there, and they all were in agreement with each other. There were no arguments of any kind.

During the days in which they prayed and worshiped, another apostle was chosen to take the place of Judas, the one who had betrayed Jesus. The name of the new man was Matthias. He joined the others in praying and waiting for the Holy Spirit. How long would they have to wait?

One day . . . two days . . . three. What did they talk about during those days? We do not know. They did not have the written Word of God as we have in the New Testament today. So they could not look into its pages to see what the Lord Jesus had taught about the Holy Spirit. But no doubt several of them remembered some of the things which they had learned about Him.

The apostle John, who wrote about it later, probably reminded the others that once, when the Lord Jesus spoke of the Spirit of God, He mentioned the wind. "The wind blows where it wants to and you hear its sound. You do not know where it comes from or where it goes. It is the same with everyone who is born of the Spirit of God." So Jesus had said to Nicodemus, as recorded in John 3:8.

Probably they all remembered that when Jesus taught them about prayer, He said, ". . . You know how to give good things to your children. How much more will your Father in Heaven give the Holy Spirit to those who ask Him?" (See Luke 11:13.) These followers of His had such a longing to get busy for Him that while they waited, they doubtless prayed earnestly for the Father to give the Holy Spirit to them–counting on His promise that He would send the Holy Spirit.

Again one would doubtless have reminded the others that the Lord Jesus had taught them that when the Holy Spirit would come, the message of Christ would flow out of them like rivers of living water. (See John 7:37-39.)

If anyone expressed fear at being left in the world without the Lord Jesus, another would have brought to his attention that they were not orphans. Jesus had promised that God the Holy Spirit would be with and in each one. They would not be alone. He would be their Comforter. (See John 14:16-26.)

If one said, "The Lord Jesus taught us so much while He was here on earth; how are we ever going to remember all of it so we can teach others?" Another would have answered, "He told us that when the Holy Spirit comes, He will teach us everything and help us to remember everything He told us." (See John 14:26.)

Four days . . . five days . . . they prayed and talked and waited. Ten days had now gone by since Jesus had returned to Heaven. It was the time of the great day of the Feast of Pentecost. Visitors from many countries of the world had come to Jerusalem to celebrate this special thanksgiving feast. Offerings of bread made out of the first sheaves of the wheat harvest were presented to God, together with sacrifices of lambs and rams and goats.

2. THE HOLY SPIRIT FILLS BELIEVERS
Acts 2:1-4

In the early morning of this special day, the believers in Jesus were together. They were all in agreement, and all were eagerly waiting for the Holy Spirit to come from Heaven. Suddenly they heard a strange noise. It sounded like a mighty windstorm. It rushed in and filled the place. Then appeared what looked like tongues of fire.

Show Illustration #6

These tongues of fire divided and rested on their heads. The disciples knew at once that these were signs, showing that the Holy Spirit had come. Immediately each person was filled with the Spirit. And because He was within them, they had the power they needed to do the work of God. Their lives were changed. Now they were strong and courageous.

3. BELIEVERS, FILLED WITH THE HOLY SPIRIT, WITNESS POWERFULLY
Acts 2:5-13

The news spread through the city that something strange had happened. Crowds who had come from every country of the world for the Pentecost feast gathered around the disciples. Peter, James, John and the others began to preach.

Show Illustration #7

The crowds listened. But they could hardly believe what they heard. The apostles, instead of preaching in the language of their homeland–Galilee–were speaking the languages of the people who crowded around them. The visitors were hearing about God and Jesus in their mother tongues. "How can these men speak in our languages? Our languages are much different from theirs."

"I know," someone mocked. "They are drunk."

"They are!" others shouted in agreement.

4. MANY PEOPLE TURN TO CHRIST
Acts 2:14-41

Show Illustration #8

Then Peter stepped forward. Once he had been a coward, and three times he had actually denied the Lord Jesus. But now he was different. He had a new power within him. He was filled with the Holy Spirit. Peter cried, "You who are visitors here as well as all of you who live in Jerusalem, listen! We are not drunk as you say. What you see happening today is what the prophet [Joel] said long ago when he declared that God would pour out His Spirit upon men. (See Joel 2:28-32.) And, as the prophet said, 'Whoever will call on the name of the Lord will be saved.' "

Peter continued, "Jesus of Nazareth, who worked many miracles and signs among you, was put to death on the cross by you. But God raised Him from the dead, just as the Scriptures foretold. And we all saw Jesus alive. Now He is in Heaven at the right hand of God the Father, and He has sent the Holy Spirit down to earth exactly as He promised. He has come today and you have seen His power. So all of you should know for sure that God made that same Jesus, whom you crucified, both Lord and Christ."

As the people listened to Peter they were deeply troubled. Was the One whom they had crucified really the Son of God? If so, they had made a dreadful mistake in putting Him to death.

Some of the men called out to Peter and to the other apostles: "What shall we do, brothers?"

Peter answered, "Repent! Turn away from your sin of rejecting Christ as the Son of God. Receive Him as your Saviour. Then your sins will be forgiven and you will receive the gift of the Holy Spirit. To prove that you have repented in your heart, be baptized in His name, so others will know you are now His."

Three thousand of those who heard Peter's message that day believed and were baptized.

The Holy Spirit had indeed come. He had entered the lives of the apostles and had begun immediately to work through them, giving them strength and courage. What a difference there would be in their lives from that moment on!

Ever since that great day at Pentecost, the Holy Spirit has been living and working within every believer. If you are a child of God, the Holy Spirit lives in you. You yourself have in you the same power the apostles had. Are you like the apostles, letting Him use you? Are you allowing Him to make you a strong, brave witness for Him? Are you telling people around you that Christ Jesus the Lord died for them?

Lesson 3
GRIEVING THE HOLY SPIRIT

NOTE TO THE TEACHER

In the first lesson we studied about the promise of the coming of the Holy Spirit. In the second lesson we learned about His actual coming. In this lesson we see that He can be pleased and that He can be grieved.

A person who is filled with the Holy Spirit will not want to grieve Him. He will want to be obedient to the Spirit. He will want to be pure. He will want to be strong in the Lord.

It can be your daily experience, dear teacher, to be strong in the Lord, to experience His power, to obey Him instead of grieve Him, to be pure in thought and word and deed. Do you believe this? You cannot be strong and pure in your own strength, for our enemy, Satan, can cause you to fall quickly. But in the power of the Holy Spirit you can be victorious.

Scripture to be studied: Acts 2:42-47; 4:32-37; 5:1-11; Ephesians 4:25-32

The *aim* of the lesson: To show that the Holy Spirit can be pleased or grieved by what we say, do or think.

What your students should *know*: The Holy Spirit knows everything about them and wants to control their lives.

What your students should *feel*: A desire to live pure, unselfish lives.

What your students should *do*: Seek to please the Holy Spirit in all they do.

Lesson outline (for the teacher's and students' notebooks):
1. Barnabas and others give to the poor (Acts 4:32-37).
2. Ananias and Sapphira decide to keep money for themselves (Acts 5:1-2).
3. Ananias and Sapphira lie to God (Acts 5:3-11).
4. Disobedience and sin grieve the Holy Spirit (Ephesians 4:30-32).

The verse to be memorized:

When He, the Spirit of truth, is come, He will guide you into all truth. (John 16:13a)

THE LESSON

Something had happened in Jerusalem, something that had never happened before. A sudden change had come over some of the men in the city. It had happened in one day, and the men could never be the same again. These men, instead of being selfish or proud or timid or quarrelsome, were full of love. They were humble and brave, powerful and kind. One of these men, Peter, spoke to a great crowd of people in a way he had never spoken before. Often before this, when Peter spoke he said the wrong thing. He had lacked wisdom. Sometimes he wasn't courageous. But now he spoke with divine power, and the things he said were right. It was as if someone else was doing the speaking.

Indeed, Someone else was doing the speaking. The Holy Spirit was speaking through Peter. The Spirit was also speaking through the other apostles. People stopped and listened to what these men said. Everyone sensed their new power.

Yes, ever since the Holy Spirit had come and filled these men on the Day of Pentecost, wonderful things had happened. Not only did the people listen to these men tell about the death and resurrection of the Lord Jesus, but hundreds, and even thousands, of them believed the words which were spoken. The listeners wanted their own lives to be changed too. Each day more people believed that Jesus Christ had died for their sins and that He had risen from the dead. They believed and were baptized. They, too, received the Holy Spirit.

The Word of God began to spread. Visitors who had come to Jerusalem for the Feast of Pentecost, and whose lives had been changed by the message, carried the news back to their own countries.

1. BARNABAS AND OTHERS GIVE TO THE POOR
Acts 4:32-37

Each day the believers in Jerusalem met together to share what God had done through them. Their hearts were so filled with the Holy Spirit and with love for one another that each meeting was a time of joy and thankfulness. They continued to praise God for all He had done. Their love was no longer for the things that they possessed. No one would say, "This is my property. This belongs to me." Instead they voluntarily shared with others what they had. They cared about the poor people. They cared so much that some sold what they owned and brought the money to the apostles. This money was used to help the poor and especially the persecuted Christians. Why did they do it? There was no law that demanded such a sacrifice. They did it because the Holy Spirit filled their hearts with love.

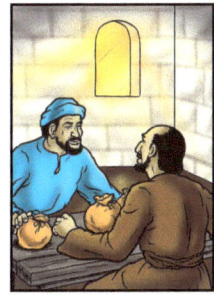

Show Illustration #9

One of the men who gave willingly was Barnabas. He was one of the believers who had been filled with the love of the Holy Spirit. He could not close his eyes to the needs of the poor people around him. Barnabas decided to help them. He could have reached into his money bag and taken out some coins to give to the poor. But no! He wanted to help with more than just a few coins. Barnabas owned some land. He sold it and brought to the apostles all the money he had received for the land.

The apostles rejoiced to see Barnabas and the other believers allowing the Holy Spirit to control and use them.

2. ANANIAS AND SAPPHIRA DECIDE TO KEEP MONEY FOR THEMSELVES
Acts 5:1-2

But Satan, the enemy of God, did not like what was happening. He did not want the people to turn to God. He did not want the believers to obey and please the Holy Spirit. He tried to work in many hearts. Some would not listen to him. Rather, they listened to the Holy Spirit. But at last Satan found two who allowed him to fill their hearts with evil desires. These two were Ananias and Sapphira.

Ananias and Sapphira were a husband and wife who professed to believe in Christ and joined with the believers. Ananias and Sapphira had heard about Barnabas and others who sold land and possessions and had given their money to help those in need. They knew the apostles were pleased. They wanted to be praised for doing some good deed. Their hearts were not filled with the Holy Spirit. They were not filled with His love. What they wanted was the praise of the apostles.

Show Illustration #10

Ananias had an idea. He talked it over with his wife, Sapphira, and she thought it was a good idea. They sold some of their land, just as Barnabas had done. Then they took the money to their home and counted out a part of it. It was this part of the money that Ananias took to the apostles. Ananias pretended that it was all the money he had received from selling his land. *Nobody will know that we have kept some of the money for ourselves*, he thought.

3. ANANIAS AND SAPPHIRA LIE TO GOD
Acts 5:3-11

Show Illustration #11

The apostle Peter looked at Ananias and at the money. But he did not praise him for what he had done. Instead Peter asked, "Ananias, why has Satan filled your heart to lie to the Holy Spirit, and to keep back part of the price of the land?"

Ananias was shocked. How could Peter know about the money he had left at home?

Peter continued, "Before you sold your land, it belonged to you; after you sold it, you could have done what you wanted to with the money. Why did you decide to make it appear as if you had brought all the money? You have lied to God, not to men." The Holy Spirit had revealed to Peter all this about Ananias.

What could Ananias say? He had no excuse. He had listened to Satan. By lying to the Holy Spirit, he had lied to God. And that very moment, God punished Ananias. Ananias fell to the ground dead. The people who heard what happened to Ananias were frightened. They realized what a terrible thing it is to lie to God.

Some young men covered the body of Ananias, carried him out and buried him. (Because of the hot climate in Jerusalem, bodies of the dead had to be buried quickly.)

About three hours later Sapphira came to Peter, perhaps wondering why her husband had not come home. She probably expected to hear the people praise her for the gift her husband had brought.

"Tell me," Peter said to her, "did you sell the land for this amount of money?"

"Yes," Sapphira answered boldly, "we sold the land for the amount we have given you."

Peter asked, "Why is it that you and your husband agreed to lie to the Spirit of the Lord? The men who have buried your husband are just outside the door, they will carry you out also."

Sapphira had lied to God. It was too late now for her to tell the truth. Immediately she fell dead just as Ananias had done.

4. DISOBEDIENCE AND SIN GRIEVE THE HOLY SPIRIT
Ephesians 4:30-32

Show Illustration #12

The young men took Sapphira out and buried her beside her husband.

It was a sad thing that happened that day. But it made the believers realize how sinful it is to grieve the Holy Spirit. Through this experience they learned that the Holy Spirit knows every thought, every word and every deed that is done. Nothing can be hidden from Him.

The Holy Spirit is just as real and powerful and holy today as He was in the days of the apostles. He wants to control your heart and give you power to live a pure, unselfish life. Remember, too, that the Holy Spirit knows everything about you. If you are a child of God, pray that you will not grieve the Spirit by acts of disobedience and sin.

Seek rather to please Him in everything you do. He will give you the power to do it.

> **NOTE TO THE TEACHER**
>
> If God were to deal today with us as He did with Ananias and Sapphira, would we still be here? Have we been guilty of pretending to be genuinely devoted to God and to His work when we are full of hypocrisy and unreality? In Ephesians 4:25-32 we read of other ways that we may grieve God the Holy Spirit. If any of these things are present in your life, confess them at once to God. If you choose to continue to grieve Him, you will not have any more power in your service for the Lord than Ananias and Sapphira had in the grave!

Lesson 4
THE HOLY SPIRIT

> **NOTE TO THE TEACHER**
>
> It is not enough to tell the Gospel story, even though we tell it simply and fully. It must be told in the power of the Holy Spirit if it is to be used by God.
>
> It is very important that you, dear teacher, know the Person and work of the Holy Spirit. He is as real a person as Jesus Christ; He is just as loving, just as wise, just as tender, just as strong and faithful, just as worthy of your surrender. The Holy Spirit is a divine Person who is always with you. The Spirit was sent by the Father into this world to be to us what Jesus Christ had been to His disciples when He was on earth. Are you completely yielded to Him? If so, it will be a great joy to you to teach some of these wonderful truths about Him.
>
> We could not possibly teach in this volume all that there is to know about the Holy Spirit. But there is so much in this lesson that you may want to divide it, making two lessons out of it. If your students would be confused by the opening part of the lesson, omit it and begin teaching with the second sentence of the eighth paragraph.
>
> In their notebooks, your students should list each of the items taught under these headings:
>
> **The Nature of the Holy Spirit**
>
> **What the Holy Spirit Is Like**
>
> **The Work of the Holy Spirit**
>
> Using the Scripture references, tell about each quality in story form, if at all possible.

The *aim* of the lesson: To teach the Person and work of the Holy Spirit.

What your students should *know*: The Holy Spirit cannot fill their lives if they have sinned.

What your students should *feel*: A desire to have the Holy Spirit fill their lives.

What your students should *do*: Ask God to reveal any sin and confess it to God.

Lesson outline (for the teacher's and students' notebooks):
1. The nature of the Holy Spirit.
2. What the Holy Spirit is like.
3. The work of the Holy Spirit.

The verse to be memorized:

When He, the Spirit of truth, is come, He will guide you into all truth. (John 16:13a)

REVIEW QUESTIONS

1. What work did Jesus tell the disciples they were to do? (*Go into all the world and preach the Gospel.*)
2. Who was to be sent from Heaven to help the disciples? (*The Holy Spirit*)
3. Where were the disciples to wait for the coming of the Holy Spirit? (*In Jerusalem*)
4. Why did the disciples need the Holy Spirit? (*For power*)
5. On what special day did the Holy Spirit come to earth? (*The Day of Pentecost*)
6. What two signs did God give to show that the Holy Spirit had come? (*The sound like a great wind and the appearance of that which looked like tongues of fire*)
7. How many people believed in Jesus Christ on the Day of Pentecost? (*About 3,000*)
8. What special thing did Barnabas do after he was filled with the Holy Spirit? (*He sold his land and gave all the money from the land to help the poor.*)
9. What was the sin of Ananias and Sapphira? (*They lied to the Holy Spirit when they acted as if they had brought all the money from the land they sold; but brought only part of it to the disciples.*)
10. Does the Holy Spirit know all our thoughts? (*Yes*)

THE LESSON

Let us suppose that a very wise man, living in another country, wanted to have many houses built in a number of our villages. He himself would have to remain at home, but he arranged with his son to come and do the building. He and his son made the plans together, so that the son knew exactly how the father wanted the houses built. Then suppose the father said, "You cannot do all the work yourself. So I want you to get others to help you. Show them exactly what I want done. Stay with them and help them until I call you back home."

But suppose before leaving, the son said, "My father is going to make it possible for you to do his work perfectly. He is going to breathe his thoughts into your mind. He has planned for one who has always been with my father and me to live within you. And although you will not be able to see him, he will be alongside you to guide you every minute."

If, in some unexplained way the man could do that, would you be afraid to do his work? Do you think that you could do exactly what he wanted done?

Suppose that someone were to ask you how you had done the work. Would you reply, "I did not do it alone; that thing helped me"?

No, I do not believe you would say that. Why not? Because it was not a *thing* that helped you. It was a person–the one who had breathed into you and had been within you and beside you.

Far more wonderful than the make-believe story, is the truth of the Word of God. God the Father sent God the Son from Heaven to earth. By seeing the Son, people knew what the Father was like. The Son taught those who followed Him to do the work of God. Then He, the perfect Son, did what no one else could ever do: He took the punishment for the sin of all the world. That punishment was death. He proved He was God the Son by rising from the dead. And when He returned to Heaven, God the Holy Spirit came to live within every believer in Christ. God has breathed His Spirit into believers. And His Spirit is a person.

Because God the Father, God the Son and God the Holy Spirit are each a part of each other, what is true of the nature of one, is true of all. In your notebook you should write these truths:

1. THE NATURE OF THE HOLY SPIRIT

1. He is *all powerful*. (See Luke 1:35; Acts 2.) On the Day of Pentecost He showed something of His great power when He changed many lives. (Show illustration #7.)
2. He is *all wise*. (See 1 Corinthians 2:9-13.) He knows everything. He knew that Barnabas told the truth. He knew that Ananias and Sapphira lied. (Show illustration #11.)
3. He is *present everywhere*. (See Psalm 139:7-12.) He is in the lives of thousands of people at one time, no matter where they are. No true believer is ever alone. He always has the Holy Spirit in him and with him.
4. He is *eternal*. (See Hebrews 9:14.) The Spirit of God always was and He always will be.

Would you like to see a picture of this wonderful person? Perhaps you are thinking, *How can we see a picture of One who is invisible?* The truth is we cannot see an actual picture of Him. But the Bible gives us some word pictures, or symbols, so that we may know what He is like. (Be sure to list–or draw–these symbols in your notebook.)

2. WHAT THE HOLY SPIRIT IS LIKE

Show Illustration #13A

1. *The wind*, or like breath. (See Acts 2:2; John 20:22.) Blow on your hand. Could you feel your breath? Yes. Could you see it? No. Neither can the wind be seen. Yet it is powerful. We can see what it does. We cannot see the Holy Spirit, but we can see the work He does in and through the lives of Christians.

Show Illustration #13B

2. Once the Holy Spirit came down like a *dove*. (See Luke 3:22.) This does not mean He now looks like a dove, but He is dove-like in gentleness, tenderness and purity.

Show Illustration #14A

3. *Oil* is also used in the Scripture to remind us of the Holy Spirit. (See Acts 10:38; Hebrews 1:9; Luke 4:18.) When David was anointed with oil, the Bible tells us, "The Spirit of the Lord came upon David from that day forward" (1 Samuel 16:13). We who are Christians are prepared to serve the Lord by the work of the Holy Spirit in our lives.

Show Illustration #14B

4. Another symbol of the Holy Spirit is *fire*. (See Acts 2:3-4.) Fire purifies. The Holy Spirit wants us to be pure. He shows us the sin in our lives. By His power we can be cleansed from sin.

Show Illustration #14C

5. The Holy Spirit is like *water*. (See John 7:38-39.) Water refreshes and quenches thirst. It also causes life to appear and makes things grow. So the Holy Spirit satisfies and refreshes the heart and life of the Christian. Each day of our lives we can continually enjoy this refreshing fountain of "living water."

Perhaps you are asking, what *work* does the Holy Spirit do? What has He done? What is He going to do? (Again, you will want to list these in your notebook.)

3. THE WORK OF THE HOLY SPIRIT

Show Illustration #15A

1. He had a part in *creating all things*. (See Genesis 1:2; Job 33:4.) He, with God the Father and God the Son, created the heaven and earth.

Show Illustration #15B

2. He gave us the *Scriptures*. He is the Divine Author. (See 2 Peter 1:20-21.) The Bible tells us that holy men of God spoke as they were moved by the Holy Spirit.

Show Illustration #15C

3. Through the Holy Spirit a person is *born into the family of God*. (See John 3:3-5, 18-21; 1 John 1:5-7; 1 Corinthians 12:13a.) Without the Lord Jesus Christ, we are separated from God. (The Bible says this is like being in darkness.) When we receive Jesus as our Saviour, our hearts are cleansed from sin by His blood. By the power of His Holy Spirit we are born into the family of God. We are no longer in darkness; we have His glorious light! (See John 8:12; 2 Corinthians 4:3-6.)

Show Illustration #16A

4. The Holy Spirit wants to *fill the life of each believer*. (See Acts 2:4; Ephesians 5:18.) There is a difference between having the Spirit of God in us and being filled with the Spirit. All believers in Christ receive the Holy Spirit the moment they are born into God's family. But it is the purpose of God for believers to be continually filled and filled and filled. In one heart you can see a little brightness, reminding us that the Holy Spirit is in that life. In the other heart the brightness is filling AND overflowing the life. Both hearts *possess* the Holy Spirit. Only one heart is *full* of the Holy Spirit.

Show Illustration #16B

5.. The Holy Spirit *guides* the Christian. We have learned that truth in our memory verse. (*Teacher:* Discuss John 16:12-15 with your students. See also Romans 8:14.) How may we be guided by the Holy Spirit? First, by *reading the Word of God*. It was the Holy Spirit who helped the men who wrote the Bible. So He helps us to understand what He caused them to write. (See 2 Peter 1:21.) Second, we can be guided by the Holy Spirit *by prayer*. You will remember that it was after Peter and the other apostles prayed, that they were filled with the Holy Spirit, and guided by Him.

(*Teacher:* If possible, bring to class a cup full of weeds and a bottle of water. Close this lesson as follows.)

What do I have here in my cup? Weeds. Now I shall add some water. Is the cup filled with water? No. The weeds must be removed before the water can completely fill the cup. Just so, we cannot be filled with the Spirit of God until the weeds of sin are removed. (Remove the weeds and fill the cup with water.) How may you be filled with the Holy Spirit?

1. Examine your life; look into your heart. See if there is anything there that does not please God.
2. Tell God about your sins. Call them by name: jealousy, pride, whatever they may be. (You know, of course, that God already knows about your sins. But He commands that you confess them to Him. See 1 John 1:8-9.)
3. Be willing to do anything that the Holy Spirit asks you to do.
4. Believe that you are filled with His Spirit, and thank Him.

www.ingramcontent.com/pod-product-compliance
Lightning Source LLC
Chambersburg PA
CBHW060806090426
42736CB00002B/171